First World War
and Army of Occupation
War Diary
France, Belgium and Germany

31 DIVISION
94 Infantry Brigade,
Brigade Trench Mortar Battery
28 April 1916 - 1 September 1916

WO95/2366/6

The Naval & Military Press Ltd
www.nmarchive.com
Published in association with The National Archives

Published by

The Naval & Military Press Ltd

Unit 10 Ridgewood Industrial Park,

Uckfield, East Sussex,

TN22 5QE England

Tel: +44 (0) 1825 749494

www.naval-military-press.com

www.nmarchive.com

This diary has been reprinted in facsimile from the original. Any imperfections are inevitably reproduced and the quality may fall short of modern type and cartographic standards.

© **Crown Copyright**
Images reproduced by permission of The National Archives, London, England, 2015.

Contents

Document type	Place/Title	Date From	Date To
Heading	WO95/2366-6 94 Brigade Trench Mortar Batty		
Miscellaneous	31st Division 94th Infy Bde Trench Mortar Battery 1916 Apr-Aug 1916		
Heading	94th Bde. 31st Div. War Diary 94th Brigade Light Trench Mortar Battery 28th April to 31st July 1916		
Heading	War Diary of 94th J.M. Battery April 28 to 31st July 1916		
Heading	94/2 Light Trench Mortar Battery April 28th 1916-May 31st 1916 Volume 1		
War Diary	Warnemont Wood	07/05/1916	15/05/1916
War Diary	Courcelles	16/05/1916	16/05/1916
War Diary	Bus	17/05/1916	17/05/1916
War Diary	Courcelles	18/05/1916	20/05/1916
War Diary	Trenches	21/05/1916	25/05/1916
War Diary	Courcelles	26/05/1916	30/05/1916
War Diary	Trenches	31/05/1916	31/05/1916
War Diary	Bertrancourt	28/04/1916	28/04/1916
War Diary	Colincamps	29/04/1916	30/04/1916
War Diary	Colincamps	01/05/1916	06/05/1916
War Diary	Warnimont Wood	07/05/1916	15/05/1916
War Diary	Trenches	16/05/1916	20/05/1916
War Diary	Courcelles	21/05/1916	25/05/1916
War Diary	Trenches	26/05/1916	30/05/1916
War Diary	Courcelles	31/05/1916	31/05/1916
War Diary	Courcelles	04/05/1916	04/05/1916
War Diary	Warnimont Wood	05/05/1916	05/05/1916
War Diary	Gezaincourt	06/06/1916	12/06/1916
War Diary	Gezaincourt	13/05/1916	13/05/1916
War Diary	Warnimont Wood	14/06/1916	30/06/1916
War Diary	Trenches	01/07/1916	01/07/1916
War Diary	E Sap	01/07/1916	01/07/1916
War Diary	Trenches	01/07/1916	04/07/1916
War Diary	Louvencourt	05/07/1916	06/07/1916
War Diary	Gezaincourt	07/07/1916	08/07/1916
War Diary	Calonne	09/07/1916	15/07/1916
War Diary	Les 8 Maisons	16/07/1916	17/07/1916
War Diary	Les 8 Maisons X Trenches	18/07/1916	25/07/1916
War Diary	Les 8 Maison	26/07/1916	28/07/1916
Heading	War Diary of 94th Trench Mortar Battery August 1916		
War Diary	Trenches	04/08/1916	18/08/1916
War Diary	Vielle Chapelle	19/08/1916	19/08/1916
War Diary	Trenches	26/08/1916	01/09/1916

WO/95/2366/6

94 Brigade Trench Mortar Batty

31ST DIVISION
94TH INFY BDE

TRENCH MORTAR BATTERY
1916 APR - AUG 1916

94th Bde.
31st Div.

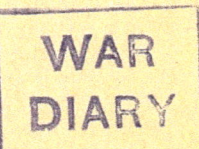

94th BRIGADE

LIGHT TRENCH MORTAR BATTERY

28th APRIL to 31st JULY 1916

Confidential

War Diary
of
94th J.M. Battery

October 24th to
1st July to 31st July
1916

Vol 1 2 3
4

Army Form C. 2118.

WAR DIARY
or
INTELLIGENCE SUMMARY

(Erase heading not required.)

Confidential

94/2 Light Trench Mortar
Battery.

April 28th 1916 — May 31st 1916
(inclusive)

Volume 1.

Army Form C. 2118.

WAR DIARY
or
INTELLIGENCE SUMMARY.
(Erase heading not required.)

Instructions regarding War Diaries and Intelligence Summaries are contained in F. S. Regs., Part II. and the Staff Manual respectively. Title pages will be prepared in manuscript.

Place	Date	Hour	Summary of Events and Information	Remarks and references to Appendices
WARREMONT WOOD	MAY 7		Church Parade. Resting. Very bad weather.	
	8		Training carried out. Route marching, gun drill etc.	
	9		Training in emplacement digging by coylping. Gun laying and ranging with dummy bombs.	
	10		Bathing parade. Gun practice and emplacement digging. O/c (2nd Lt Hudson) proceeds on leave of absence. Weather fine.	
	11		Digging practice.	
	12	11 a.m	Visit by Commander in Chief. Emplacement digging and ranging practice. Training of four men as reinforcements commenced. 895. Pte Crawshaw promoted L/cpl. 226) Pte Marshall G.) Returned to 1084 Pte Jackson S.) 14th taken on 861 . Ashton G.A.) 14th Y.L. no Troop G.) S.Y.L strength of 405 . Barraclough T.) mountable. 662 . Sharp G.) battery.	Lt Potter 2/L
	13		Very bad weather. Practice in ranging with dummies.	
	14		Church parade. Duel weather. O/c/n Review orders to move to Courcelles on 15th inst.	

Army Form C. 2118.

WAR DIARY
or
INTELLIGENCE SUMMARY.
(Erase heading not required.)

Instructions regarding War Diaries and Intelligence Summaries are contained in F. S. Regs., Part II. and the Staff Manual respectively. Title pages will be prepared in manuscript.

Place	Date 1916	Hour	Summary of Events and Information	Remarks and references to Appendices
COURCELLES	MAY 15	11 a.m.	2/Lieut Potts moved with one section to COURCELLES, via BUS, BERTRANCOURT. Out billeted under canvas in field N of COURCELLES. 7/R m Sergt and remaining section arrive with transport 94/1 go into trenches. Report on covering of green envelopes, nothing military found in them.	
	16	12.30 p.m. 2.30 p.m.	Our artillery bombarding. Gun practice etc. Receive one hand cart for use of battery. Forward 13 shell jackets to D.A.D.O.S. for alteration. Forward one gun to Vacherrauval School for (use of reinforcements.) Very fine weather.	
BUS	17	2 p.m.	Battery give a demonstration before G.O.C. 31st Division and 14th Bn York L.co. Very good shooting. Brilliant weather.	
COURCELLES	18		Ranging practice from trenches W of COURCELLES. Brilliant weather. 9 p.m. C.O. (Lieut Hereden) returns from leave.	
	19		Rout march and gun practice.	
	20	12.45	Took over in trenches from Battery 94/1. Have two guns in and one in support. Emplacements all along a Camel tramway to the left off tramway Avenue (K 29 A) 20 yards behind front line. 11th Bn East Lancs. holding front line. Weather brilliant. Line very quiet.	MAP REFCE Nelmitim 57D NE 3 & 4.
		8.30 a.m. 9.30 a.m.	Fired 100 shells bursting on enemy's front line at K 29 B 23 (range 300) and K 29 D 1200 (range 270). Fired two rounds "Regd target" could not estimate damage.	

1577 Wt.W10791/1773 50,000 1/15 D. D. & L. A.D.S.S./Forms/C. 2118

WAR DIARY or INTELLIGENCE SUMMARY

Army Form C. 2118.

Place	Date 1916	Hour	Summary of Events and Information	Remarks and references to Appendices
TRENCHES	MAY 21		Weather very fine. Line quiet. Good observation post established near officers dugout. 8.15 p.m. fired four shots on to enemy's front line. Good shots but could not estimate damage.	
	22		Weather very fine. Very quiet. 4.15 p.m. fired three shots on to enemy's front line. Immediately after our shot they fired five odd bangs in quick succession which went over the emplacements to our right. Dug another emplacement at K 29 A 75 but were not allowed to use it owing to proximity of Off head. Enemy commenced a bombardment at 10.20 p.m. damaging our front line.	
	23	3 a.m	Fired two shots, range 290. Very effective. Line quiet all day.	
	24	2.45 a.m	Enemy fired rifle grenades at our front line. We replied with two shots which dropped in their front line trench. Quiet after.	
		4.20 p.m	We fired two shells at 4.20 (one dud), range 290, and at 4.50 reducing the range 15 yards. Our gun returned from Yackerenne.	
	25	3.15 a.m	We fired four shots, two at 275 yards and two at 290. Could not estimate damage. Slight mist, observation difficult.	
		2 p.m	Relieved by Battery 94/1. Relief carried out in order. Handed over 129 rounds of ammunition. Marched to camp at Couvrelles.	

Army Form C. 2118.

WAR DIARY
or
INTELLIGENCE SUMMARY.
(Erase heading not required.)

Place	Date	Hour	Summary of Events and Information	Remarks and references to Appendices
COURCELLES	MAY 26	NIGHT 10.40 to 11.20	Inspections and gun training carried out. Provide ration carrying party for 94/1 battery. And Carrying of reinforcements for Stokes guns. South section of our line bombarded.	
	27		Gun training and providing fatigue party.	
	28		do.	
	29		do. (13 H Y & L)	
	30		Lieut L.O.R. Huggard attached to this battery for fire days. Took over from 94/1 battery in the trenches. Relief successfully completed at 10.15 p.m. Our sector — MATHEW COPSE (K 29 A) to MAIRNE ST (K 28 d 35). 14th Bn YORK & LANCS holding front line. Weather very fine. Line quiet.	(Traf Rifles HEBUTERNE 57D N.E. 3 & 4 (front of))

Army Form C. 2118.

WAR DIARY
or
INTELLIGENCE SUMMARY

(Erase heading not required.)

Place	Date	Hour	Summary of Events and Information	Remarks and references to Appendices
TRENCHES	1916 MAY 31	3.25 a.m.	Fired two rounds at K.29.t.22 at German front line. First on air burst, the second bursting on parapet.	
		8.30 a.m.	Enemy fired a number of canister bombs. We replied with Trench Mortars.	
		4.30 p.m.	Dug an emplacement in COPSE TERRACE, left Sector, and commenced to fire, but enemy must have observed us. Enemy artillery ranged and blew trench in so we withdrew the gun. One man slightly hurt with dirt in OBSERVATION WOOD.	

J. Potter
J. P. 2/4

Army Form C. 2118.

94/1 T.M.B. Original

WAR DIARY
INTELLIGENCE SUMMARY
(Erase heading not required.)

Instructions regarding War Diaries and Intelligence Summaries are contained in F. S. Regs., Part II. and the Staff Manual respectively. Title Pages will be prepared in manuscript.

Place	Date 1916	Hour	Summary of Events and Information	Remarks and references to Appendices
BEATRICOURT	Apl 28	2 a.m.	Battery moved to COLINCAMPS.	
COLINCAMPS	29	9 a.m.	Places 2 mortars in positions in trenches. Found it difficult to locate good positions for Stokes' Mortars. 2 Guns in reserve at COLINCAMPS.	
"	30		Digging Emplacements in trenches.	
"	May 1		Locals & favourable sites for Gun emplacements in WICKER TRENCH	
	2		Digging Emplacements in trenches.	
	3		do	
	4		do	
	5	6 a.m. to 10:30	Relieved by 92/2 Battery. Moves to WARNIMONT WOOD	
WARNIMONT WOOD	7		Training	

9th/11 TMB
Original

WAR DIARY
or
INTELLIGENCE SUMMARY

Army Form C. 2118.

Place	Date	Hour	Summary of Events and Information	Remarks and references to Appendices
WARNIMONT WOOD	May 8		Training	
"	9		Training Brigade class in Stokes' Mortars	
"	10		do. class continued to 13th inst	
"	14		Training	
"	15		74/1 Battery moved to COURCELLES, also 2 Stokes in trench on LEFT of Divisional Line. 2 mortars in reserve at COURCELLES.	
TRENCHES	16		Bombardment in COPSE TRENCH first on enemy front line that was seen to fall on the parapet and Strench. Barrage fire difficult to maintain Rifles on enemy trench for rifle grenades and counter bomb.	
"	17		ditto	
"	18		Quiet. No firing	

94/ TMB.
Original

Army Form C. 2118.

WAR DIARY
or
INTELLIGENCE SUMMARY
(Erase heading not required.)

Instructions regarding War Diaries and Intelligence Summaries are contained in F. S. Regs., Part II. and the Staff Manual respectively. Title Pages will be prepared in manuscript.

Place	Date 1916	Hour	Summary of Events and Information	Remarks and references to Appendices
TRENCHES	July 20	3 am	Fired on enemy trenches. Relieved by 94/2 TMB. at 1 p.m. Moves back to COURCELLES.	
COURCELLES	21		Training personnel to 24th inst.	
"	25	4 pm	Relieves 94/2 Battery in trenches.	
TRENCHES	26		Digging new positions in COPSE TRENCH.	
"		3 p.m.	Registered 3 shots from new position on Rouchon	
"	27		Quiet. No firing.	
"	28	p.m. 7.30	Fires on enemy trench in retaliation for renades etc.	
"	29		Fire from new position in COPSE TRENCH Range 500s.	
"	30	p.m.	Quiet.	
"		9.30	Relieved by 94/2 Battery	
"			Moves back to COURCELLES.	

94/1 T.M.B.
Original

Army Form C. 2118.

WAR DIARY
INTELLIGENCE SUMMARY
(Erase heading not required.)

Instructions regarding War Diaries and Intelligence Summaries are contained in F. S. Regs., Part II. and the Staff Manual respectively. Title Pages will be prepared in manuscript.

Place	Date	Hour	Summary of Events and Information	Remarks and references to Appendices
COURCELLES	May 31		Training continues to June 3rd	
"	June 3		Moved to WARNIMONT WOOD	
WARNIMONT WOOD	4		Marched to GEZAINCOURT. Found the transport a good bit to pull to keep up with Brigade Column	
GEZAINCOURT	5 6		Training. Route march of trucks.	
"	7		to	
"	8		Demonstration by 94/1 and 94/2 Batteries. Lessons learnt — not much though Wire not well cut enough. Some to trench. Batteries completely by the Acting Brig. Gen. on display.	
"	9			
"	10		Inspection	
"	11		Battery stables near attachment	
"	12		to	
WARNIMONT	13		Moved to WARNIMONT WOOD. Coy is in bad condition	

94/1 T.M.B. and 94/2 funnelled into 94/2 T.M.B. under command of Capt. Watson Batteries 94/1 and 94/2

94th T.M.B Original

WAR DIARY or INTELLIGENCE SUMMARY

Army Form C. 2118.

(Erase heading not required.)

Instructions regarding War Diaries and Intelligence Summaries are contained in F.S. Regs, Part II and the Staff Manual respectively. Title Pages will be prepared in manuscript.

Place	Date 1916	Hour	Summary of Events and Information	Remarks and references to Appendices
WARNIMONT WOOD			Training class in Stokes Mortars	
do	15		Moved to AUTHIE.	
do	16		From June 16th to 29th spent time in training T.M.detachment as to act as reinforcements and ammunition carriers. Preparing and carrying mortar ammunition (3600 rounds) into trenches, to the places to be placed in D and E saps	
do	30	4.30 a.m	Moved to TRENCHES. Each T.M. Section in D sap with 2 offrs & men to be in the front trench. T.M.2 Section in E sap with 3 offrs. of T.M. mortars in front trench. T.O. & Section in reserve.	
EDEN TRENCH	July 1	a.m 7.20	Everything ready at 3 a.m July 1st Delivered a hurricane bombardment on German Front Line until zero 7.30am to 7 secs fired 50 rounds and T.O.2 Section 600 rounds	
E.sap.		p.m 7.20	Received a message from A/gt 1/5 York & Lancs. Regt (in E sap) to the effect that the Yeomany were bringing up & consolidating	

9th T.M.B.
(Original)

WAR DIARY
or
INTELLIGENCE SUMMARY
(Erase heading not required.)

Army Form C. 2118.

Instructions regarding War Diaries and Intelligence Summaries are contained in F.S. Regs., Part II. and the Staff Manual respectively. Title Pages will be prepared in manuscript.

Place	Date	Hour	Summary of Events and Information	Remarks and references to Appendices
TRENCHES	1916 July 1	7.10 am	On this front Light Infantry left trenches first and S.A.A. The mortar in each fives about 100 rounds on the first shots taking effect. Found it impossible to advance owing to infantry attack being held up also on account of heavy machine gun fire.	
		11.0 am	Received orders to 1 and 2 Sections to retire to EDEN TRENCH leaving No 3 Section in D.20. This section retired at 5 am July 2nd to EDEN TRENCH. Called the roll and made up casualty returns. One officer and 3 men killed, 19 men wounded. Carrying guns and ammunition/my own ? to front line.	
"	2			
"	3		Relieved at midnight and marched to LOUVENCOURT	
LOUVENCOURT	4		Cleaning mortars and equipment. Addressed by Lieut. Newton Wodehouse and Captain Campbell.	

Army Form C. 2118.

9th TMB
Original

WAR DIARY
or
INTELLIGENCE SUMMARY

(Erase heading not required.)

Instructions regarding War Diaries and Intelligence Summaries are contained in F. S. Regs., Part II. and the Staff Manual respectively. Title Pages will be prepared in manuscript.

Place	Date	Hour	Summary of Events and Information	Remarks and references to Appendices
LOUVENCOURT	1916 Aug 6	10 AM	Marched to GEZAINCOURT.	
GEZAINCOURT	7		Training.	
"	8		Marched to FREVENT, entrained for STEENBECQUE, marched to CALONNE.	
CALONNE	9		Training.	
"	10		" Battery addressed by Earl O'Gowran.	
"	11		Training continued until 15th	
"	15	11 AM	Marched to LES 8 MAISONS.	
LES 8 MAISONS	16		No. 1 and 2 Sections continued training to the 27.8.15. No. 3 Section took over positions in trenches from 185 TMB in front of NEUVE CHAPELLE. No. 3 Section fires an average per day registering new positions	

2449 Wt. W14957/M90 750,000 1/16 J.B.C. & A. Forms/C.2118/12.

Army Form C. 2118.

WAR DIARY
or
INTELLIGENCE SUMMARY

(Erase heading not required.)

Instructions regarding War Diaries and Intelligence Summaries are contained in F. S. Regs., Part II. and the Staff Manual respectively. Title Pages will be prepared in manuscript.

4th T.M.B.
Original

Place	Date	Hour	Summary of Events and Information	Remarks and references to Appendices
LES 8 MAISONS Y TRENCHES	1916 July 19		(3) Below retaliates on German front line for trench mortar.	
		19	ditto. One shot notices to throw up a parapet.	
			Trench bombs etc.	
			Below continued firing on enemy front line.	
		20	do	
		21	do	
		22	do. Relieved by (1) section at 8 p.m.	
		23	do. Below registered S9. (2) below registered in front line.	
			No 1. no 3. sections training.	
			shots from new positions in front line.	
		24	(2) Below fires 38 rounds on German line retaliation	
			for enemy rifle etc. Took up new positions tonight of	
			west front 116 T.M.B.	
		25	(1) Below registered German new position no	
			right sector. 2 extra aeroplane flares sent up, meaning	
			'all'	

2449 Wt. W14957/M90 750,000 1/16 J.B.C. & A. Forms/C.2118/12.

94th T.M.B.
Original

WAR DIARY
or
INTELLIGENCE SUMMARY
(Erase heading not required.)

Army Form C. 2118.

Place	Date	Hour	Summary of Events and Information	Remarks and references to Appendices
LES 8 MAISONS	July 1916		(2) Action fired 71 rounds on enemy's line.	
	29		(3) Action retaliated with 85 rounds on enemy's line.	
			for prevalence etc. Relieved by 93rd T.M.B. at 6 pm	
	28		94th T.M.B. continues training until Aug 4th	

2449 Wt. W14957/M90 750,000 1/16 J.B.C. & A. Forms/C.2118/12.

Confidential

War Diary

of

8th Trench Mortar Battery

August 1916.

V

94" T.M.B.
Original

Army Form C. 2118.

WAR DIARY
or
INTELLIGENCE SUMMARY
(Erase heading not required.)

Instructions regarding War Diaries and Intelligence Summaries are contained in F.S. Regs., Part II. and the Staff Manual respectively. Title Pages will be prepared in manuscript.

Place	Date	Hour	Summary of Events and Information	Remarks and references to Appendices
TRENCHES	1916 Aug 4		Took over positions in trenches from the 93" T.M.B. Places guns in NEUVE CHAPELLE Sector.	
		5	Fired 156 rounds on enemy's lines. Blew in many direct hits and also blew up something resembling a wheel, possibly a trench mortar. Enemy replied with T.Ms. One man wounded.	
		6	Fired on enemy front and support lines. Obtaining direct hits.	
		7	Fired 33 rounds. Hits observed. Machine gun emplacement believed to have been hit at S.11.a.4.4.	
		8	With Stokes guns strenuous in retaliation to rifle grenades. One man wounded.	
		9	Fired 25 rounds every ½ to avoid torpedoes etc. One man wounded.	
		10	Fires on enemy front and support lines. Damage done to his parapet.	

94" T.M.B
Original

Army Form C. 2118.

WAR DIARY
or
INTELLIGENCE SUMMARY
(Erase heading not required.)

Instructions regarding War Diaries and Intelligence Summaries are contained in F. S. Regs., Part II. and the Staff Manual respectively. Title Pages will be prepared in manuscript.

Place	Date	Hour	Summary of Events and Information	Remarks and references to Appendices
TRENCHES	Aug 11		Replies to enemy's rifle grenades, with 20 rounds, now taking effect.	
	12		Fires 11 rounds. Co-operates with artillery on enemy's line. Replies to rifle grenades with success.	
	13		Day of fire. Enemy unusually quiet.	
	14		Replies to enemy's rifle grenades. Front and support line. Fires on enemy group. Replies throughout the day to rifle grenades.	
	15		Fires on enemy's wiring line. Destrs. obtained.	
	16		Replies on enemy's firing in co-operation with artillery. Dis'm'd damage to German line. Runs of pits 157	
			Enemy used 6 T.M. doing no damage.	
	17		Counter firing. Retaliates on German line to ry'y to grenades etc.	
	18		Releases 6 by 16" T.M.B at 7.50 a.m. North of NEUVE CHAPELLE.	

WAR DIARY or INTELLIGENCE SUMMARY

Army Form C. 2118.

94" T.M.B
Original

Instructions regarding War Diaries and Intelligence Summaries are contained in F.S. Regs., Part II. and the Staff Manual respectively. Title Pages will be prepared in manuscript.

(Erase heading not required.)

Place	Date	Hour	Summary of Events and Information	Remarks and references to Appendices
NEUVE CHAPELLE	Aug 19		Training until Aug 26th	
TRENCHES	26		Took over emplacements in front line, S. of NEUVE CHAPELLE. From 185" T.M.B. Registered position	
	27		Fired 131 rounds on German front line inflicting some damage to his parapet	
	28	5 pm 9 pm	Combined with the artillery in cutting enemy's wire. Fired 340 rounds. Observers and patrols reported wire well cut and 5 damaged.	
	29	4 am 5.0	Carried out same operation as yesterday. Firing 235 rounds on wire and 30 rounds at enemy's trench. Retaliated to fire from S.W. Weather bad.	
	30		Weather bad. Enemy very quiet. Rain.	
	31	4.0 5.0	Fired 19 rounds. Enemy's wire. 56 rounds fired, doing much damage.	
Left	1 am 1.05		Fired 19 rounds from 2 guns to cover wire of Bayside Redan "1A" at wire to cut wire during a raid at 1 am. Our fire believed to have stopped shells in the midst of a German working party. During the day enemy quiet	

G.H. Hudson Capt.
O.C. 94" T.M.B -

www.ingramcontent.com/pod-product-compliance
Lightning Source LLC
Chambersburg PA
CBHW081506160426
43193CB00014B/2607